Bush Theatre

STATUES
by Azan Ahmed

Statues was produced by Two Magpies Productions in association with the Bush Theatre and premiered at the Bush Theatre, London, on 9 October 2024.

STATUES

Cast

Yusuf, Mustafa & others	Azan Ahmed
Omar & Khalil	Jonny Khan

Creative Team

Director	Esme Allman
Set & Costume Designer	Cara Evans
Lighting Designer	Rachel Sampley
Sound Designer & Composer	Holly Khan
Engagement Producer & Assistant Director	Maryam Shaharuddin
Movement Director	Hamza Ali
Production Manager	Adam Jefferys
Stage Manager	Lois Sime
Associate Producer	Eve Allin

Originally developed by Nuu Theatre.

Supported using public funding by the National Lottery through Arts Council England.

Cast

Azan Ahmed | Yusuf, Mustafa & others

Azan Ahmed (he/him) is an award-winning actor, poet & playwright.

As an actor, recent credits include: *We Go Again* (BBC Three); *10 Nights* (Omnibus & tour); *Van der Valk* (ITV); *The Father and the Assassin* (National); *Count Abdulla* (ITVX); *The Tempest* (Globe).

His debut play *Daytime Deewane* (Half Moon & tour) won the 2023 Off West End Theatre Award for Best Writing. He is currently being mentored by Roy Williams as part of the Hampstead Theatre INSPIRE cohort. Azan is an alumnus of Apples and Snakes Writing Room, Almeida Young Company and Bush Young Company. He also produces *Deen & Dunya*.

Jonny Khan | Omar & Khalil

Jonny Khan (he/him) is an actor, writer and DJ living in South London. His theatre work includes: *The Tempest* (RSC); *Vanishing Room* (New Diorama / English Theatre Frankfurt); *Assembly: The Teachers Play* (Almeida Theatre); *Anthem* (Bush Theatre); *A Very Special Guest Star* (Omnibus); *United* (New Vic). On television he has appeared in *Sister Boniface* (BBC). As a writer, Jonny is the recipient of the Bloom Bursary with Bush Theatre and is currently under commission with Camden People's Theatre.

Creative Team

Azan Ahmed | Writer

Azan Ahmed (he/him) is an award-winning actor, poet & playwright.

As an actor, recent credits include: *We Go Again* (BBC Three); *10 Nights* (Omnibus & tour); *Van der Valk* (ITV); *The Father and the Assassin* (National); *Count Abdulla* (ITVX); *The Tempest* (Globe).

His debut play *Daytime Deewane* (Half Moon & tour) won the 2023 Off West End Theatre Award for Best Writing. He is currently being mentored by Roy Williams as part of the Hampstead Theatre INSPIRE cohort. Azan is an alumnus of Apples and Snakes Writing Room, Almeida Young Company and Bush Young Company. He also produces *Deen & Dunya*.

Esme Allman | Director

Esme Allman (she/her) is a director, theatre-maker, facilitator and poet from South London. She built her theatre practice in a participatory context at the Young Vic, Clean Break and Cardboard Citizens. She directed the R&D of *Statues* by Azan Ahmed (Pit Theatre, Barbican) as part of Barbican Open Labs (2022). She also directed *To The People* by John Dinneen and Alex Urwin (April 2022). She has been an assistant director for *OUT* by Ray Young (touring Spring 2024), *Cinderella* by Danusia Samal (Brixton House, December 2023), *Alice in Wonderland* (RADA Vanbrugh Theatre, August 2023) and *Run It Back* (Talawa Theatre and Hackney Showroom 2018). Previous theatres and creative organisations she has worked with include Arts Ed, the Barbican Centre, Brixton House, Fevered Sleep, Lyric Hammersmith, Kings Theatre, Theatre Royal Stratford East, Sydenham Arts, and the Robert Bosch Foundation in Berlin.

Cara Evans | Set & Costume Designer

Cara Evans (they/she) is a London-based performance designer. Cara graduated in Design for Stage from the Royal Central School of Speech and Drama and worked as a reader at the Royal Court.

Theatre credits includes: as Designer or Co-Designer, *Feral Monster* (National Wales); *Sleepova* (Bush Theatre); *Dear Young Monster* (Bristol Old Vic Studio); *The Living Newspaper* (Royal Court); *Sirens* (Mercury Colchester Studio); *Get Dressed!* (Unicorn); *Queer Upstairs* (Royal Court); *Body Show* (Soho); *Sylvia* (English Theatre Frankfurt); *It's a Motherf**king Pleasure* (National Tour); *Ugly Sisters*

(New Diorama); *SK Shlomo: Breathe* (Royal Albert Hall); *F**king Men* (Waterloo East); *The Beach House* (Park); *Love Bomb* (National Youth Theatre); *Baba Joon* (Swansea Grand Studio); *Bright Half Life* (King's Head); *The Misandrist* (Arcola); *Instructions for A Teenage Armageddon* (Southwark Playhouse); *Blanket Ban* (New Diorama, UnTapped); *A Different Class* (Queen's Hornchurch); as Associate Designer for Chloe Lamford, *Teenage Dick* (Donmar School's Tour).

Rachel Sampley | Lighting Designer

Rachel Sampley (she/her) is a London-based lighting and video designer.

Her previous work includes *Barrier(s)* (National Theatre); *Perfect Show for Rachel* (The Barbican); *The Great Gatsby* (Immersive Everywhere); *The Suspicions of Mr Whicher* (The Watermill); *Bossy* (Zoo Co/Southbank Centre); *Cassie and the Lights* (59E59, Off Broadway, NY); *Opal Fruits* (Bristol Old Vic/Pleasance Edinburgh); *The Great Gatsby* (Immersive LDN/Seoul, Korea/Theatre Clwyd); *Wreckage* (Turbine); *Breeding* (King's Head – nominated for an Off West End Theatre Award for Lighting Design).

She has an MA in Advanced Theatre Practice from the Royal Central School of Speech and Drama.

Holly Khan | Sound Designer & Composer

Holly Khan (she/her) is a British/Guyanese composer, sound designer and multi-instrumentalist, creating scores for theatre, film and installation.

Most recent theatre work includes *Our Country's Good* (Lyric Hammersmith); *Sam Wu is not Afraid of Ghosts* (Polka); *Sylvia* (English Theatre Frankfurt); *A Child of Science* (Bristol Old Vic); the Olivier-nominated *Blackout Songs, This Much I Know, Biscuits for Breakfast* (Hampstead Theatre); *Tess* (Turtle Key Arts / Sadler's Wells); *Dreaming and Drowning* (Bush); *I Really Do Think This Will Change Your Life* (Colchester Mercury); *Duck* (Arcola); *Northanger Abbey, Red Speedo* (Orange Tree Theatre); *The Invincibles* (Queen's Theatre Hornchurch); *Unseen Unheard* (Theatre Peckham); *Laughing Boy, Jules and Jim* (Jermyn Street Theatre); *Mansfield Park* (The Watermill); *The Beach House* (Park); *For A Palestinian* (Bristol Old Vic/Camden People's Theatre - nominated for an Off West End Award for Best Sound Design); *Amal Meets Alice* (Good Chance Company/The Story Museum); *Kaleidoscope* (Filskit Company, Southbank Centre/Oxford Playhouse).

Hamza Ali | Movement Director

Hamza Ali (he/him) is an interdisciplinary movement artist. He directs, coaches, facilitates, and performs movement for performance.

Movement direction credits include: *10 Nights* (UK Tour); *Duck* (Pleasance/Arcola); *Going For Gold* (Chelsea Theatre); *For One More Day to Live* (Theatre Peckham); and *Daytime Deewane* (Half Moon Theatre).

He was the Resident Director for Dante or Die's *Kiss Marry Kill* (UK Tour). Original productions including: *Bhai* (The Place); and *1518* (Greenside). He has facilitated for theatres including LUNG and The Kiln and has taught at the National Youth Theatre where he is an associate artist. He is currently a resident artist at artsdepot. A recipient of the Embassy Scholarship, he graduated with an MA in Movement from the Royal Central School of Speech and Drama, where he directs movement as a visiting professional.

Maryam Shaharuddin | Engagement Producer & Assistant Director

A youth & community facilitator, Maryam Shaharuddin (she/her) co-creates theatre with participants in the UK and Malaysia.

She has delivered workshops & performances at a range of organisations including Angel Shed, Kiln Theatre, Almeida Theatre, Bush Theatre, PositivelyUK, Company Three and The National Theatre. She is also an Associate Artist at Coney, focusing on a practice of playful activism with communities. Her assistant directing credits include: *Daytime Deewane* (Half Moon Theatre); and *Duck* (Arcola). She has worked as an engagement producer for *This Might Not Be It* and *Statues* (Bush Theatre). She is also currently a mentor for Tamasha's Creative Wellbeing Lab, sharing her practice in arts and health. Joy and play are at the heart of her practice in creating inclusive, socially engaged theatre. Maryam is especially passionate about making work that celebrates and elevates the stories of Muslim Women.

Adam Jefferys | Production Manager

Adam Jefferys (he/him) is a Lighting Designer and Production Manager from Essex. Previously, he was the Technical Manager of the New Diorama Theatre.

Recent work includes: *Foreverland* (Southwark Playhouse); *Playfight* (Summerhall Festival Theatre); *I Love You, Now What?*

(Park); *The End, Communion, My Father's Fable, Elephant* (Bush Theatre); *The Bleeding Tree, Under The Kundè Tree* (Southwark Playhouse); *The Great Privation* (Theatre503); *The Olive Boy* (UK Tour); *Murder In The Dark* (UK Tour); *It Is I, Seagull* (UK Tour); *Soon, Pilot* (Summerhall); *Philosophy of The World* (Cambridge Junction); *After The Act, War & Culture* (New Diorama); *Project Dictator* (New Diorama & Edinburgh); *Jekyll and Hyde* (Derby Theatre); *Everything Has Changed* (Tour & Edinburgh); *Dorian* (Reading Rep).

Lois Sime | Stage Manager

Lois Sime (she/her) trained in Stage Management as Guildhall School of Music and Drama. Previous credits include: *The Last Word* (Marylebone Theatre); *For Tonight* (Adelphi); *Brassed Off* (Aberystwyth Arts Centre); *You Bury Me* (Paines Plough); *Mother Goose* (Hackney Empire).

Eve Allin | Producer

Eve Allin (she/her) is a producer for theatre. She is Executive Producer at Broccoli Arts, a production company making work for/by/about lesbian, bisexual and queer people who experience misogyny. Broccoli productions include: *Tender, This Might Not Be It* (Bush Theatre); *Salty Irina* (Paines Plough Roundabout, Summerhall); *Before I Was a Bear* (Soho Theatre).

Eve was Associate Producer at Soho Theatre for *Super High Resolution* and *Boys on the Verge of Tears*. Independently, she is the producer for the internationally award-winning *Civilisation* by Jaz Woodcock-Stewart; *work.txt* by Nathan Ellis and *WRESTLELADSWRESTLE* by Jennifer Jackson. Eve is a Stage One supported producer.

TWO MAGPIES PRODUCTIONS

Two Magpies Productions is a new production company from maatin, an award-winning writer focused on telling Muslim stories.

First and foremost, we believe in the urgent need for a radical transformation of both the creative arts industry and the world, towards a more just and more equal future for all.

Further, that we live in a society that is structurally anti-Muslim, which therefore must be given consideration to in all areas of our work.

This is at the heart of everything we do.

We prioritise those from marginalised and minoritised identities, to create opportunities for those who remain underrepresented in the creative arts.

In particular, we desire to centre Muslimness, for all its breadth, range and meaning to those who identify with it, and look to increase the participation of Muslims in all areas of the creative process.

We will only make work in a safe environment that protects workers, upholding the highest standards of professionalism, labour rights, dignity and access.

Bush Theatre

We make theatre for London. Now.

For over 50 years the Bush Theatre has been a world-famous home for new plays and an internationally renowned champion of playwrights.

Combining ambitious artistic programming with meaningful community engagement work and industry leading talent development schemes, the Bush Theatre champions and supports unheard voices to develop the artists and audiences of the future.

Since opening in 1972 the Bush has produced more than 500 ground-breaking premieres of new plays, developing an enviable reputation for its acclaimed productions nationally and internationally.

They have nurtured the careers of writers including James Graham, Lucy Kirkwood, Temi Wilkey, Jonathan Harvey and Jack Thorne. Recent successes include Tyrell Williams' *Red Pitch*, Benedict Lombe's *Shifters*, and Arinzé Kene's *Misty*. The Bush has won over 100 awards including the Olivier Award for Outstanding Achievement in Affliate Theatre for the past four years for Richard Gadd's *Baby Reindeer*, Igor Memic's *Old Bridge*, Waleed Akhtar's *The P Word* and Matilda Feyişayọ Ibini's *Sleepova*.

Located in the renovated old library on Uxbridge Road in the heart of Shepherd's Bush, the Bush Theatre continues to create a space where all communities can be part of its future and call the theatre home.

> '**The place to go for ground-breaking work as diverse as its audiences**' EVENING STANDARD

bushtheatre.co.uk
@bushtheatre

Artistic Director	Lynette Linton
Executive Director	Mimi Findlay
Associate Artistic Director	Daniel Bailey
Deputy Executive Director	Angela Wachner
Development & Marketing Assistant	Nicima Abdi
Development Officer	Laura Aiton
Head of Marketing	Shannon Clarke
Head of Development	Jocelyn Cox
Associate Dramaturg	Titilola Dawudu
Finance Assistant	Lauren Francis
Resident Director & Young Company Director	Katie Greenall
Technical & Buildings Manager	Jamie Haigh
Assistant Venue Manager	Rae Harm
Head of Finance	Neil Harris
Marketing Officer	Laela Henley-Rowe
Associate Producer	Nikita Karia
Community Assistant	Joanne Leung
Senior Producer	Oscar Owen
Assistant Venue Manager	Simon Pilling
Senior Technician	John Pullig
Event Sales Manager & Technician	Charlie Sadler
Venue Manager (Theatre)	Ade Seriki
Press Manager	Martin Shippen
Community Producer	Holly Smith
Literary & Producing Assistant	Laetitia Somè
Marketing Manager	Ed Theakston
Assistant Venue Manager (Box Office)	Robin Wilks
Theatre Administrator & Executive Assistant	Chloe Wilson
Café Bar Manager	Wayne Wilson

DUTY MANAGERS
Sara Dawood, Molly Elson, Thomas Ingram, Madeleine Simpson-Kent & Anna-May Wood.

VENUE SUPERVISORS
Antony Baker, Addy Caulder-James, Stephanie Cremona, Emma Chatel, Zea Hilland, Nzuzi Malemda, Roy Mas, Jacob Meier & Louis Nicholson.

VENUE ASSISTANTS
Javine Aduganfi, Doridan Bavangila, Charlotte Binns, Will Byam-Shaw, Pyerre Clarke, Daniel Fesoom, Matias Hailu, Bo Leandro, Maya Li Preti, Ishani McGuire, Khy Matinez, April Miller, Ed Mendoza, Carys Murray, Chana Nardone, Jennifer Okolo, James Robertson, Ali Shah & Nefertari Williams.

BOARD OF TRUSTEES
Uzma Hasan (Chair), Mark Dakin, Kim Evans, Keerthi Kollimada, Lynette Linton, Anthony Marraccino, Jim Marshall, Rajiv Nathwani, Kwame Owusu, Stephen Pidcock, Catherine Score & Cllr Mercy Umeh.

Bush Theatre, 7 Uxbridge Road, London W12 8LJ
Box Office: 020 8743 5050 | Administration: 020 8743 3584
Email: info@bushtheatre.co.uk | bushtheatre.co.uk

Alternative Theatre Company Ltd
The Bush Theatre is a Registered Charity
and a company limited by guarantee.
Registered in England no. 1221968 Charity no. 270080

THANK YOU

Our supporters make our work possible. Together, we're evolving the canon and creating a bolder, more diverse, and representative future for British theatre. We're so grateful to you all.

MAJOR DONORS
Charles Holloway OBE
Jim & Michelle Gibson
Georgia Oetker
Cathy & Tim Score
Susie Simkins
Jack Thorne
Gianni & Michael Alen-Buckley

SHOOTING STARS
Jim & Michelle Gibson
Cathy & Tim Score
Susie Simkins

LONE STARS
Jax & Julian Bull
Clyde Cooper
Adam Kenwright
Anthony Marraccino & Mariela Manso
Jim Marshall
Georgia Oetker

HANDFUL OF STARS
Charlie Bigham
Judy Bollinger
David des Jardins
Sue Fletcher
Thea Guest
Elizabeth Jack
Simon & Katherine Johnson
Joanna Kennedy
Garry & Lorna Lawrence
Phyllida Lloyd & Kate Pakenham
Vivienne Lukey
Aditya Mittal
Sam & Jim Murgatroyd
Mark & Anne Paterson
Martha Plimpton
Nick & Annie Reid
Bhagat Sharma
Joe Tinston & Amelia Knott
Dame Emma Thompson

RISING STARS
Elizabeth Beebe
Martin Blackburn
David Brooks
Catharine Browne
Anthony Chantry
Lauren Clancy
Richard & Sarah Clarke
Caroline Clasen
Susan Cuff
Matthew Cushen
Anne-Hélène and Rafaël Biosse Duplan
Austin Erwin
Kim Evans
Mimi Findlay
Jack Gordon
Hugh & Sarah Grootenhuis
Sarah Harrison
Uzma Hasan
Lesley Hill & Russ Shaw
Davina & Malcolm Judelson
Mike Lewis
Lynette Linton
Michael McCoy
Judy Mellor
Caro Millington
Rajiv Nathwani
Yoana Nenova
Stephen Pidcock
Miguel & Valeri Ramos Handal
Karen & John Seal
James St. Ville KC
Jan Topham
Kit & Anthony van Tulleken
Evanna White
Ben Yeoh

CORPORATE SPONSORS
Biznography
Casting Pictures Ltd.
Nick Hern Books
S&P Global
The Agency

TRUSTS & FOUNDATIONS
Backstage Trust
Buffini Chao Foundation
Christina Smith Foundation
Daisy Trust
Esmée Fairbairn Foundation
The Foyle Foundation
Garfield Weston Foundation
Garrick Charitable Trust
Hammersmith United Charities
The Harold Hyam Wingate Foundation
Idlewild Trust
Jerwood Foundation
Martin Bowley Charitable Trust
Noël Coward Foundation
The Thistle Trust

And all the donors who wish to remain anonymous.

If you are interested in finding out how to be involved, please visit **bushtheatre.co.uk/support-us** email **development@bushtheatre.co.uk** or call **020 8743 3584**.

STATUES

Azan Ahmed

Acknowledgements

Thank you to Lynette Linton, Daniel Bailey, Katie Greenall, Gurnesha Bola, Ellie Horne, Ben Quashie, Becky Lyle, Nuu Theatre and Barbican Centre for believing in this play from the very beginning. To Esme Allman for your vision, brilliance and unwavering support. To maatin (Two Magpies Productions) for your dedication, kindness and holding us all together. To Mr Khan, for your insight, honesty and fighting the good fight.

To the incredible company: Eve Allin, Adam Jeffreys, Cara Evans, Rachel Sampley, Holly Khan and Lois Sime. And to everyone at Bush Theatre and Nick Hern Books for all their support.

To Maryam Shaharuddin and Hamza Ali, it is truly a pleasure to watch your artistry blossom.

To my fellow actor Jonny Khan, whose generosity of spirit lit up the rehearsal room.

To Luke Reilly and Christina Shepherd, for their belief and guidance.

To Raja Roy Chowdhury, for telling me to keep writing.

To Bex Smith, for being a pillar of warmth.

To everyone who held me in the immediacy of my grief and those who continue to do so.

Above all else, the praise and thanks are ultimately to Allah, whom I owe every single thing to and whom I pray accepts this play and its intentions.

A.A.

*For my mama, Afshan Ahmed,
the best teacher I'll ever know.
For my baba, Oneil Ahmed,
the greatest storyteller I'll ever know.
For my brothers, Zahran and Faizan Ahmed,
who redefine joy each time they smile.*

Allah, you gave us a language
where yesterday & tomorrow
are the same word. Kal.

A spell cast with the entire
mouth. Back of the throat
to teeth. Tomorrow means I might

have her forever. Yesterday means
I say goodbye, again.
Kal means they are the same.

Fatimah Asghar, 'Kal'

Characters

PRESENT DAY

YUSUF, *Muslim. Twenty-six. Third-generation British Pakistani. English teacher. Mustafa's son*

KHALIL, *Muslim. Seventeen. Second-generation British Pakistani. Year 13 A-level student*

DOLLY AUNTY, *Muslim. Seventy-seven. First-generation British Pakistani. Yusuf's great-aunt*

PAUL, *white English. Headteacher at Yusuf and Khalil's school*

1996

MUSTAFA, *Muslim. Nineteen. Second-generation British Pakistani. Aspiring rapper. Omar's best friend*

OMAR, *Muslim. Nineteen. Second generation British Pakistani. Aspiring DJ. Mustafa's best friend*

Notes

This play can be performed by two actors, with the following doubling:

Actor A: Yusuf/Mustafa/Paul/Dolly Aunty
Actor B: Omar/Khalil

" " indicates when Yusuf is speaking to another character

– indicates a hesitation

/ indicates overlapping interruption

[ ] indicates lines thought and not spoken

This text went to press before the end of rehearsals and so may differ slightly from the play as performed.

Scene One

We are in the living room of a council flat in South Kilburn. Specifically, this is number 50 Wordsworth House on the South Kilburn Estate. There is a Persian rug and the living room is littered with moving boxes, stack of unopened post. In the centre lies an unopened suitcase. The boxes are not empty, but not full. During the first scene, YUSUF *should clear up some of the clutter. Maybe there are three moving boxes. One to give to charity, one to bin, one for* YUSUF *to keep.*

Lights up on YUSUF. *He is wearing a collared shirt with a vest underneath and chinos. Since he is not at work, his shirt may be open. He is in the house, so is not wearing shoes. Socially he wears Nike Blazers, Converse or Adidas Sambas. At work he may wear a sleek but easy pair of Chelsea boots.*

YUSUF. Packing.

Noun: the act or process of packing something.

Adjective: American slang for carrying a gun, especially on a regular or habitual basis.

Don't panic. I don't have a gun. See? No gun.

Nothing exciting here. No gun… or maybe there is? Nah nah like maybe he had one here?

YUSUF *looks through boxes.*

Imagine returning to your childhood home to discover that your dad, your baba, hid a gun in the flat the whole time. Or nah imagine yeah what if, during this process of packing, peering through cupboards and drawers my fingertips slide across a secret lever, leading down to a cave where I find cape, cowl and spandex. Now THAT would be exciting! What if?

What if I didn't have to imagine stories where my baba is interesting – was interesting.

When you grow up on a block like this, stories are a lifeline. Comics, novels, poetry – stories transport you to possibilities less grey, less concrete.

YUSUF*'s phone buzzes.*

Five missed calls from Dolly Aunty.

YUSUF *picks up three items and randomly assigns them to the 'charity', 'bin' and 'keep' boxes. This activity is ongoing for the rest of the scene.*

Haven't been back to South Kilburn for years. Live in North Finchley now, calmer. Nice greenery, cute community fayres. They even have a flowery sign that says: 'Welcome to North Finchley'.

Closest thing SK has to any kind of welcome is a yellow square on a lamp post: 'CCTV now in operation'. I wonder what they'll rename the blocks. On the SK estate, they're all named after writers. Dickens House, Austen House and our block, Wordsworth House. Same block where C Biz is from, same block where that guy jumped out of the eighth floor when his flat got raided.

Phone buzzes.

Instagram. Bare messages. All condolences. Friends, ex-girlfriend, even the bully from school. Can't reply to them now, I'm packing.

YUSUF *goes back to packing but again his phone buzzes.*

Dolly Aunty again. Asking where I am. Dolly Aunty ain't even my aunty, she is – was Baba's aunty but refuses to be called daadi even though she's bare old.

Phone buzz. YUSUF *puts the phone on flight mode.*

Flight mode. There.

YUSUF *looks at how much he has to pack. Maybe he has items in hand, unsure where they should go.*

Got two weeks to pack this flat up. Normally you get a month when a council tenant. But they're regenerating the block, so they want it done quick time.

He randomly assigns three items to 'charity', 'bin', 'keep'.

I'm packing the flat because my dad, my baba is gone. Baba di-passed three days ago. Funeral was three hours ago. We do funerals quick. Can't decide when Eid is, but funerals?

YUSUF *clicks his fingers to resemble speed.*

Regimented. I like that efficiency. Islamically, you have three days of mourning then you move on.

Clicks fingers.

And I am moving on. Start my dream job tomorrow, Head of English at my old secondary school, youngest Head of English in the school's history! I'm nervous. Which is why *I* shouldn't be lumped with all this – this packing. But he is – *was* my baba so I have to. Even though I barely knew the man.

What can I tell you about Baba…his name was Mustafa. His wife – my mum – left us when I was eight and he spent all his time sat there like a statue, watching Geo News and reruns of *Fresh Prince*. I lived with him for eighteen years and that's all I know. So, I have no idea what to do with all the clothes, cutlery and carpets. It should be Dolly Aunty here not me.

YUSUF *randomly assigns another two items to the 'charity' and 'bin' boxes. He then picks up a jai namaaz* (prayer mat). *After a moment, he places it in the 'keep' box.*

It was sudden apparently. That's what Dolly Aunty said when she called with the news. In his sleep, subhanallah. That's supposed to make me feel better right? When you play Death Top Trumps in your head. 'Went in his sleep' that's good. 'We had a non-existent relationship' that's bad.

YUSUF *takes another item out to sort. It is a '90s cassette player. He's baffled.*

He hated music? He used to mute songs on TV adverts! (*Thinking.*) For old Quran tapes maybe? Can probably sell this on Vinted to some hipster.

YUSUF *places the cassette player down. He looks at it. The Grief Music creeps in.*

Baba was hard work. His sighs and shoulder slumps replaced sentences. Baba was a man of few words, many grunts. His silence was deafening. Hard work, man, he was rigid like stone. And I'm an English teacher who wears chinos...I'm soft. By Baba's standards, by SK's standards I'm soft. And that's fine.

But these past three days, I feel too soft. My limbs are wobbly. I get these waves where time bends, my heart swells and I feel like I'm gonna spill or melt or float all at the same time. So I hold it down until I feel solid again.

Maybe it's the flat, being reminded how much hard work he was. Maybe it's my body settling into the idea Baba is forever past-tense, and all I have to remember him is the silence.

The Grief Music swells. YUSUF *reaches his arm out and grabs an imaginary pang, shoving it back inside of him. Packing it. As he does so the music fades out.*

Maybe it's the kebab I had last night. It'll pass inshallah, just have to finish packing.

YUSUF *shakes it off and rummages for another three items to sort. After throwing the first two items, he unveils a green-and-white '90s nylon track jacket. He laughs at the thought of it belonging to his baba.*

No way.

YUSUF *smells the jacket. It's his baba's scent.*

Oud. It is his.

YUSUF *inspects the jacket. He can feel something in the pocket. He pulls out two cassette tapes.* YUSUF *inspects one of the tapes. It should feel like Hamlet holding Yorick's skull.*

Must be the Quran tapes.

YUSUF *attempts to put the cassette in the player, but he's Gen Z.*

(*Holding cassette.*) Bismillahirrahmanirraheem.

Finally, he manages it. He presses play and walks back to the suitcase. The tape player blasts out a '90s hip hop track.

Astaghfirullah! Ey, it's quite good still.

Wait… what?

YUSUF *approaches the cassette player, rewinds and presses play. His suspicion is right. He rewinds and presses play one more time to be sure.*

Track One

The music from the cassette now fills up the space, we are transported to 1996 and a charismatic MUSTAFA *appears wielding a mic, with DJ* OMAR *at the decks.*

Rap. Italics are pre-recorded chorus.

MUSTAFA.
Check one two my name is Double MC
Coming at you live with DJ OG
1996 we feelin' free
Brown bruddas blessing the mic it's obscene

Fuck a wordsmith I'm a baato ka raj
Leading the charge with my moo and my haat
With my pad and pen, dil on my sleeve
Ain't no MCs stopping me

Word to your ummi imma make cash money
Rhymes so sublime taste better than a curry
Rhymes so sublime make you think twice
'Bout how you view, skin like mine

STATUES

Raised in a block named after great writers
Dickens Wordsworth William Blake
Double MC a natural-born fighter
Spit my way to the top of the food chain

Flow like a butterfly sting like a bee
Yeah you know me, Double MC
Think I'm wack I'll spin your jaw clean
Yeah you know me, Double MC

British Asian second generation
Read Shakespeare and I think in Urdu
British Asian no punctuation
Aaja sunno here is my truth

Call me Hamlet, method to my madness
Macbeth no brudda born of a woman can test
Measure for measure Double MC the best
Spittin' like a storm call me The Tempest

Double MC like a young Ali
Flow like a butterfly sting like a bee
Heavy beats by DJ OG
SK to the world everybody know we

Dazzle with the mic make all the honeys look
Handling the verses collecting big purses
Slip past stereotype snap the hook
Step to me imma show you where the hearse is

Flow like a butterfly sting like a bee
Yeah you know me, Double MC

Come from a place where we despise jakes
And the roads around us have sealed our fate
Shoot Up Hill, Kilburn High Road
Script been written on how they want us to go

But me 'n' OG say hell no
Me 'n' OG got mad flow
Desi bro poetry in the soul
The white man, don't want you to know

Power, grace the beauty in your face
They try bring us down in so many ways
Smelly, dirty, our family are swarms
And all we are good for are corner shop stores

Bhenchod! We are so much more
Double MC gonna make 'em all see
Modern-day Mushiree can't shush me
Double MC gonna flip the bird
If any white man try tell me my worth!

Yeah you know me, Double MC
Yeah you know me, Double MC

MUSTAFA *and* OMAR. YOOO!!!

The boys do a complicated handshake they've done for years.

One take! They call me Mr One Take! Did you feel that? Ey send them this one, yeah.

OMAR. Yeah.

MUSTAFA. Send it today.

OMAR. Yeah.

MUSTAFA. We about to get signed, G!

OMAR. Mustafa, it's just a demo track. They never said they'd sign us.

MUSTAFA. I know I know, I'm just getting excited... but once they listen. And hear the vibes... they're gonna sign us innit?

Beat.

OMAR (*excited*). Yeah.

The boys do the handshake again.

MUSTAFA. Ey Omar, I can proper see it, man. Record deal with Sony, albums, sold-out crowds Wembley Arena, Glasto all bumpin' our tunes!

OMAR. Slow down, rudeboy, we don't have even have an EP, how we gonna sell out Wembley?

MUSTAFA. We – oi that rhymed you know. Come on, MC in disguise yeah? Ey drop a lil freestyle.

MUSTAFA *rushes over to* OMAR, *putting the mic near his mouth.*

OMAR. Nah man.

MUSTAFA. Come on, G, it's just me and you don't be shy.

OMAR. Mus[tafa].

MUSTAFA *doesn't budge.* OMAR *clears his throat, attempts to freestyle, bottles it.* MUSTAFA *is cracking up until he sees* OMAR*'s embarrassment.*

See this is why I stay behind the decks.

MUSTAFA. Yeah but what you can do, mix that bhangra with the bass – wicked. Like a magician.

OMAR. Do you think we can actually do it? Get a record deal?

MUSTAFA. Course, rudeboy! *We* are the missing link. Asian underground music has stayed underground coz there ain't been no lyricists. But us? Brown Jazzy Jeff and Fresh Prince.

OMAR. Wicked.

MUSTAFA. Plus your cousin works at Sony so we're in.

OMAR. Not my cousin.

MUSTAFA. You said /

OMAR. / My cousin Neha – her husband's brother's girlfriend is Bally Sagoo's assistant, he just signed with Sony.

MUSTAFA. Husband's brother's girlfri– That sounds way less impressive.

OMAR. Nah trust. Bally meets with the execs all the time. They signed him to get more Asians on the label. I'll send this track today, they'll listen.

MUSTAFA. Inshallah.

OMAR. Inshallah.

SCENE TWO 15

OMAR. Same time tomorrow yeah?

MUSTAFA. Nah, G, it's a full house tomorrow, Dolly Aunty's coming over. My family's going Pakistan next week though, we can record then?

OMAR. Oh shit.

MUSTAFA. What?

OMAR. Tape's still recording.

MUSTAFA. Quick shut it / off then!

OMAR. / Yeyeye chill!

The boys scramble over to the decks/tape recorder to shut it off.

A rewind sound. A school bell rings. Back to present day, YUSUF *stacks/sorts boxes and buttons his shirt.*

Scene Two

YUSUF *is at work. A mixed comprehensive secondary school in South Kilburn.*

YUSUF. Risk.

Noun. One syllable. The possibility of something bad happening.

We all squeeze into the staffroom for a briefing.

My mind is doing a madness. Keep pinching myself to focus. My Baba was… a rapper?!

Don't act weird, Yusuf, it's your first day at school. Literally.

Nah but seriously. My baba. Baba the living statue was a charismatic, cool, clever MC? It doesn't make any sense. I don't need it to make sense, I don't even want to think about it. But I can't shake it. His bars and righteous energy are so loud. Can't pack it away.

Paul, the headteacher. When did he get here? Fix up.

YUSUF *holds down a pang. He makes himself presentable.*

Don't do anything risky.

Paul is steamrolling through the staff briefing with the confidence only a privately educated white man can.

PAUL. In a bustling, vibrant and soulful borough like this –

YUSUF. I think he means ends.

PAUL. It is our duty to identify individuals at high-risk.

YUSUF. He means people of colour I think? Risk of what?

PAUL. And prevent them from further… risk of radicalisation.

YUSUF. Oh he means Muslims.

I speak posh. Went Oxford on a bursary, thought I was gonna be the British Mohsin Hamid, until I wasn't. Then I did a PGCE.

Risk. A noun. A stain. One syllable giving birth to many raised eyebrows.

PAUL. Odd remarks or behaviours should be reported. The quicker we act, the safer pupils are from risk. We must protect the youth.

YUSUF. I have a theory. Anyone who refers to young people as 'the youth' shouldn't be in charge of young people. I almost say this, then I remember it's my first day.

PAUL. We'd also like to welcome our new Head of English, and former pupil of this very school – Yusuf Malik!

YUSUF. Why do non-Muslims always go hard on the pronunciation? Strong but so wrong. Again, I don't say this. I know Paul sounds dodgy, but I think his heart's in the right place. He hired me, right?

Paul rambles about prayer times being inconvenient with lesson times but my mind wanders to what Double MC would make of Paul. Probably call him a pasty red-faced gora. Baba's voice sounded like fireworks on that tape; I can hear it clapping back at this fossil. But then my heart sinks because I never got to know that voice. How can I miss someone I barely knew?

Then I remember –

YUSUF *holds down a pang.*

I didn't tell work that Baba is gone.

YUSUF *holds down a pang.*

That silly little tape doesn't change a thing.

YUSUF *holds down a pang.*

I'm Head of English now. It ain't worth the risk.

School bell rings.

Scene Three

YUSUF*'s classroom.*

YUSUF. I'm a good teacher. My last inspection they said I was 'modern, approachable and passionate'. But today is not going as planned.

I try to conjugate verbs with Year 8. But I can't stop thinking about Baba's wordplay.

I try to dissect World War Two Poetry with Year 10. But all I can hear and see is… Double MC… his righteous energy.

I'm starting to rhyme. He's proper in my head!

Grief Music comes in.

I'm trying to pack it in but it's not working. These thoughts keep slowing me down then speeding me up. They swirl around my stomach, making my empty belly full. My legs like jelly.

I can't stop thinking 'What if I got to know him?' Baba – Double MC. Would we get on? He was so passionate. Hearing that, growing up with a lyricist – would it have made me take writing more seriously? He was so passionate. What happened? I'm not annoyed that Baba was a rapper. I'm annoyed that he was good and didn't tell me.

If I knew him, I would have –

YUSUF *holds down an almighty pang. Something has shifted. Temporary clarity. Grief Music is gone.*

Everything goes quiet. My legs are solid. Everything's solid. I've got this second skin, spread tight, covering and binding my limbs like cement. My heart steadies.

Come on, Yusuf. Baba is past-tense. You're Head of English now.

School bell rings. YUSUF *acknowledges it is slightly harder to move with this second skin.*

"Right, Year 13! Great to meet you all. I'm Mr Malik, your new English teacher."

They chuck their bags down, click pens and slap chewing gum across teeth. But it doesn't faze me. I'm solid.

"Let's get our playtexts out. You all should've read this over the summer. Act One, Scene Two please."

KHALIL *clambers in late, half-folded prayer mat in hand. Palestine badge on his backpack and blazer. He takes his seat without saying a word, stuffing the prayer mat in his backpack.*

YUSUF. "Hi. Why are you late?"

KHALIL. Coz I'm late.

YUSUF. "What's your name?"

KHALIL *kisses his teeth.*

A few minutes ago, this attitude would've made me go all wobbly. But I'm solid, like cement.

YUSUF *walks over to* KHALIL *and offers his hand.*

"I'm Mr Malik."

KHALIL *turns away pointedly.* YUSUF *smiles.*

"I already know your name from the register, I'd like you to introduce yourself."

Beat. YUSUF *turns back to the centre of classroom.*

"You can't be late to class, alright?"

KHALIL. I can't be late for my prayers, alright?

YUSUF. "I know. But I managed to pray Zuhr and turn up on time." I read the shortest surahs. "If this were a job interview and you turned up late, sweaty, shirt untucked, tie loose – do you think I'm gonna hire you? Manage your time, don't make it any easier for people to reject you."

KHALIL. Thanks for the speech, new guy, but it ain't my fault the prayer room is all the way on /

YUSUF. / "Ground-floor caretaker's cupboard. I know."

KHALIL. Innit! Wait. How'd you know that – I swear you're new?

YUSUF. "I went to this school when I was younger. Was the same back then."

KHALIL. You went here?

YUSUF. "Yes."

KHALIL. Did you go uni then?

YUSUF. "Yes, I went to Oxford."

KHALIL. Rah they let *you* in Oxford?!

YUSUF. I didn't need to say Oxford. But it's a compulsion. I gotta name-drop it. It's a flex. I'm aware. But it shows him what's possible.

"Course they let me in. Got my grades and wrote a solid personal statement. I can look at yours if you like?"

KHALIL. Swear? I was gonna get ChatGPT to write mine.

YUSUF. "Happy to help. But I need your name first."

KHALIL. Khalil, sir.

YUSUF. Khalil. Paul told me about this kid. Pretends he hates English but won the Key Stage Four poetry competition a couple years ago.

KHALIL. Ey sir, can I pray Zuhr in your classroom then?

YUSUF *considers, then almost reluctantly.*

YUSUF. "Yeah sure."

Hurriedly shifting attention to the rest of the class.

"Year 13, sorry about that. Playtexts please. Act One, Scene Two."

YUSUF *gets out his playtext.*

It's *Hamlet*. We're doing *Hamlet*. The dramatic irony isn't lost on me.

"Who can tell me what's happened so far?"

KHALIL. Hamlet's dad is dead. He's bare depressed. Lost and frustrated. Proper doom 'n' gloom.

The Grief Music creeps in. YUSUF *abruptly packs another pang.*

YUSUF. "Before we start, do we all know what a soliloquy is?"

KHALIL. 'Course we know what a soliloquy is.

YUSUF. "Some people might not know, it's a big word, soliloquy, three syllables!"

KHALIL. Four syllables.

YUSUF. "Good, now I know you're listening. Can you tell us what it means?"

KHALIL. Soliloquy is when a character talks directly to the audience. Shares their honest feelings.

YUSUF. "Thank you, Khalil. Now we all feel more equipped right? We all share an understanding of language, have a seat at the table, we all" /

KHALIL. / Ey calm down sir this ain't *Dead Poets' Society*!

YUSUF. "You watched *Dead Poets' Society* yeah?"

KHALIL. Nah.

YUSUF. "But you just" /

KHALIL. / My mum was watching it. I just happened to be walking past innit.

YUSUF. "For two hours, eight minutes?"

KHALIL. I was doing a lot of walking that day still.

YUSUF. Eventually they all settle and take turns reading passages and things feel normal. We're comparing all of Hamlet's soliloquies, charting his journey of grief.

KHALIL. Ey, sir.

YUSUF. "Yeah?"

KHALIL. Hamlet. He's –

KHALIL *makes a sound which suggests Hamlet's mad.*

YUSUF. "What do you mean?"

KHALIL. He's a bookie guy innit.

YUSUF. "What do you mean by that?"

KHALIL. I mean he's bookie.

YUSUF. "You can't say 'bookie' in your exam."

KHALIL. Why not?

YUSUF. "Because you – [can't]. There are more intelligent, sophisticated words to show you understand the text. Let's try it. What do you mean by 'bookie'?"

KHALIL. Like… Hamlet's not right.

YUSUF (*nods*). "One word to describe him?"

KHALIL. Shaky.

YUSUF. "Shaky?"

KHALIL. Shaky… like not on solid ground.

YUSUF (*nods*). "Why does he feel shaky?"

KHALIL. Coz he's searching.

YUSUF. "Searching for what?"

KHALIL. His dad.

YUSUF. "But his dad's gone."

KHALIL. He's still searching for him. Searching for purpose. You can proper see it in the second soliloquy. He calls upon the forces of hell to hold his heart. Bookie!

YUSUF. "He calls upon heaven as well."

KHALIL (*studying his playtext*). Yeah yeah he does still. He's lost innit! Doesn't know who to turn to.

YUSUF. "How do we know that?"

KHALIL. You can tell he's lost coz… the rhyme and rhythm, the metre, isn't uniform. All over the place.

YUSUF (*impressed*). This is really /

KHALIL. / Oi, sir, I got it! Hamlet in one word yeah?

YUSUF. "Yeah."

KHALIL. Radical.

Beat.

YUSUF. "What?"

KHALIL. Hamlet is radical. A radical. Mad extreme

YUSUF. "I don't know if" /

KHALIL. / Nah nah he is. He starts off lost and shaky. Then coz he's vulnerable, he's radicalised by his father's ghost!

YUSUF. He knows he shouldn't be saying that word. It's risky. "I think" /

KHALIL. / My man forgets his old life and commits himself to the ghost's cause: "thy commandment all alone shall live". Tell me this ain't textbook radicalisation.

YUSUF. It's my first day, I can't have him slinging that word around. Can't have Paul think I let him sling that word around.

Grief Music rises. YUSUF *holds down a pang.*

"Great analysis, Khalil, why don't we stick to language that will help in your exam. Let's use the term 'tragic hero'."

KHALIL. But why?

YUSUF. "Because that's what Hamlet is. A tragic hero."

KHALIL. He's not a hero.

YUSUF. "He's one of the greatest characters in literature, every actor wants to play him."

KHALIL. You're begging it. Hamlet isn't your boy, relax.

YUSUF. Oh I get it. I'm the new teacher, he's testing me, seeing if I'll crack. Nah mate, I am solid. "I'm just trying to teach English, Khalil."

KHALIL. And I'm speaking English. Hamlet is a radical.

YUSUF. "Tragic hero."

KHALIL. So you're tryna teach me that a posh white boy who harasses Ophelia and shanks three man is a hero?

YUSUF. "Look, Khalil."

KHALIL. / If Hamlet is a hero, then by your logic that means every radical can be seen as a hero innit? Anyone standing against injustice. Palestinians, Sudanese, Congolese.

YUSUF. "Khalil, this isn't history, this is English Literature."

KHALIL. I answer your questions, can't you answer mine?

YUSUF. "Can we stay on topic, please?"

KHALIL. This guy thinks I'm going off topic.

YUSUF. "I'm not 'this guy'. I'm sir."

KHALIL. Aight 'sir', what makes Hamlet different? How come his extremism is validated?

YUSUF. I don't have time for this.

KHALIL. Ey, sir, you're rattled. Sticking up for Hamlet won't make you his boy you know.

YUSUF. "Khalil."

KHALIL. If Hamlet was real he'd probably hate you, 'sir'.

YUSUF. "Khalil! Headteacher's office, now!"

School bell rings.

Scene Four

Back at Mustafa's flat (50 Wordsworth House). YUSUF *moves boxes.*

YUSUF. I've spent the evening aggressively cooking. Chicken biryani. Not for me, for the pack of random aunties and uncles in Baba's living room. They're here to perform Afsos.

'Afsos.' Urdu word. Verb and noun. Meaning sorry, regret, condolences.

I don't need Afsos. Islamically, we're done with that. I can hear Dolly Aunty cackling as they all trade stories about Baba.

I mash onions to drown them out. Drown my mind out. Khalil doesn't get it! The rules are different for him, me, most of that class. Work twice as hard. Be twice as professional. He can't just turn up late, disrespect Hamlet and say words like… I've never sent a student out before. Firm but fair. Paul said, in this school, you have to be firm but fair.

YUSUF *shakes it off.*

It was just a rough start. I'm a good teacher, just couldn't concentrate properly. Had Baba in my head. Every time I think about him my brain feels like mashed onions. How could someone so confident become so silent? Man up, Yusuf. I just need to listen to that second tape, chuck it in the bin pile and be done with it. As soon as these lot leave that's what I'll do. No more distractions. Back to normal.

I serve the biryani.

DOLLY AUNTY. Oh Yusuf! I told you to use the good plates.

YUSUF. "I've packed them, Dolly Aunty. Let's just use the paper ones."

They don't even say thank you for cooking. They just –

YUSUF *mimics an aunty eating and chewing open-mouthed, obnoxiously loud.*

And in between all the –

YUSUF *mimics an aunty eating and chewing open-mouthed, obnoxiously loud.*

They keep talking about Baba.

Grief Music starts to build.

Stacking adjectives like Jenga. Baba was cheeky, badmaash, charming. The more they speak, the more I see how much he meant to them. Their emotion seeps into my skin, slipping past the cement. I'm starting to wobble.

Grief Music swelling.

Cheeky, badmaash, charming. What's mad is I can't even deny it, I've heard it. With each story that pours out of them

I start to feel it. Baba's righteous energy. Suddenly I'm flooded with all these thoughts and there's no cement to stop them.

Did they know he rapped? If not why not? If so why won't they tell me? Why didn't he tell me?

YUSUF *holds down a pang. Becomes more solid.*

I bring chai and biscuits. Just power through.

They tell me to read Surah Mulk, Surah al Waqi'ah and Surah Yasin but I don't listen. I don't cry when they cry. I don't let it get to me. Baba is past-tense.

DOLLY AUNTY. You know they killed her because she was going to convert?

YUSUF. Dolly Aunty is holding a Princess Diana mug which I PACKED AWAY.

"Can we not touch the boxes please."

She rummages like a raccoon. Taking out a notepad and something small, I can't see. Aunties, man. No respect for boundaries.

"This stuff needs to go. So let it go."

She slips the small object into her handbag.

"What is that?"

DOLLY AUNTY. Why do you care? Mr Let It Go. This new generation. Everything throw. Everything Mary Kondo.

YUSUF. "It's Marie Kondo."

DOLLY AUNTY. Array Kondo Shondo, bakwaas! All of these are memories. Why don't you want to see your baba?

A stare-off between the two.

YUSUF. "What's the point, Dolly Aunty? What is the point of romanticising who he was, who he could've been when he was never that to me. He's gone. Baat khattam."

Their jaws are on the floor. I think I'm the first Pakistani in the history of this dunya to stand up to elders.

SCENE FOUR

Eventually they all shuffle out with an ice-cream tub of biryani each... except Dolly Aunty.

DOLLY AUNTY. We haven't even read Quran yet.

YUSUF. "I'll read later."

Beat.

DOLLY AUNTY. You know why we do Afsos, beta?

YUSUF. Free food and drink?

DOLLY AUNTY. You have this one image of your baba. But we have full album. So we make mazak, eat his favourite dish, laughing shaughing telling stories so you have full album. Makes it easier.

YUSUF. "I don't have time to make imaginary albums Aunty. Work, packing the flat" /

DOLLY AUNTY. / Array flat shat! In Islam, soul never dies. You must know your baba's soul. So you can reach him with Dua, with Quran. Afsos is not three days, beta, it is for life, and Allah has given us verses specifically for our parents. You need to reach him, meri jaan.

YUSUF. She stares waiting for me to speak. But my heart is in my throat and I'm scared of spilling. Her phone buzzes. Her son is outside. She shuffles out.

DOLLY AUNTY. Allah Hafiz, meri jaan. I'm here okay? Give me call on Whatsup. It's good to talk.

YUSUF *walks over to the open box with the notepad on top. He picks up the notepad to pack it back in but...*

YUSUF (*reading*). 'Property of Mustafa Malik. Don't fucking touch!'

Lyrics. Scribbled on every inch.

YUSUF *reads. Smiles. He puts the notepad back on top of the box. He does not pack it. He walks towards the cassette player. Holding up the second tape with wonder, he goes to put it in the cassette player but backs away. He is now holding up the cassette with frustration.*

(*Indicating cassette.*) *This* is the problem! Before this I was... What's the point? Doesn't change anything. He's not coming back is he? Baat khattam.

Beat. YUSUF *smirks to himself.*

If I press play now and keep listening, keep wondering, searching for Baba, I'll end up like Hamlet! He obsessed over his grief and look what happened to him! It doesn't matter that I didn't know the cheeky charming MC. Been fine without him. Graduation, PGCE, Head of English without him. I shove my heart back down, I shove all the adjectives and stories they dumped down until I can't feel any of it. Until my limbs, my eyelids feel impenetrable. Like stone.

YUSUF *holds down a huge pang. His body is a lot more tense and heavy.*

YUSUF *firmly moves/shoves/stacks boxes.*

Scene Five

School.

YUSUF. Numb. Adjective. Deprived of sensation

Paul gives his staff briefing. Something about internal exclusion.

Classes shuffle in, shuffle out. I'm calm. I don't even feel wobbly any more. I don't feel anything. I forget I have fingers until I see them typing. It's harder to move, but I'm here for it. Efficiency.

So I conjugate 'slay' and other verbs with Year 8. Compare World War Two poetry and drill with Year 10. Nothing fazes me, I'm solid.

Year 13 shuffle in. No Khalil. No hello. No good afternoon.

Gets his copy of Hamlet *out.*

SCENE FIVE

"Anyone wanna read?" Silence. They're all frozen. For a moment, I think they're all statues.

"Alright, different question, anyone seen Khalil?"

Silence again. They can barely look at me! Firm but fair.

"Not talking isn't going to get you anywhere. Talking too much, being disruptive like Khalil, is going to get you sent out. I'm here to guide you. I know what it's like, I've literally sat where you've sat. People look at you like you won't succeed coz you come from a place like this. But the more we talk, the more you arm yourself with literature, vocabulary, you'll have enough syllables to smash through what anybody thinks."

Silence. Damn. That was a good teacher speech, like that was *Dead Poets' Society*, *Coach Carter* levels. Somehow the lesson ends with more silence than it began with. It's the end of the day, but before I head home I stop by Paul's office.

"Sorry to bother you, just wanted to check in about Khalil. Year 13, he's been absent for a week."

PAUL. Ah yes. Khalil.

YUSUF. Again with the pronunciation.

PAUL. I've been meaning to tell you. Khalil has been moved to internal exclusion.

YUSUF. "What?"

PAUL. You sent him to my office, did you not?

YUSUF. "I did do that, yeah."

PAUL. I found his comments quite alarming.

YUSUF. "Alarming?"

PAUL. Yes. He used the R-word.

YUSUF. "The" /

PAUL. / Radical. Come on, Yusuf, keep up! Which of course, in his context, referred to radicalisation.

YUSUF. This is not happening.

PAUL. I don't know how it worked in your old school, but we must keep an eye on these things. In recent months Khalil's behaviour has become increasingly concerning. He has been praying frequently .

YUSUF. "There are five daily pra–" /

PAUL. / And when you sent him here, I noticed aggressively political badges on his blazer and backpack. I had no choice but to take it further and escalate.

YUSUF. "Why didn't you consult me? I'm his teacher."

PAUL. And I'm the headteacher. Quite frankly I'm surprised you, out of all our staff, didn't spot these concerns sooner. It's our duty in the public sector to report these matters.

YUSUF. "Report what? He hasn't done anything."

PAUL. Yet. He hasn't done anything yet. Khalil has been referred to Prevent.

YUSUF. That word takes all the wind out of me.

PAUL. The officers at Prevent and Channel will help course-correct his behaviour. You did the right thing sending him to me, Yusuf.

Beat. YUSUF *tries to absorb this. He is uneasy. He is back at the flat.*

YUSUF. I wobble back to the flat in what feels like one breath. Everything is speeding up and slowing down again. Keep thinking. About everything I could have said. I feel heavy but also like jelly.

YUSUF *starts shoving Grief Pangs down.*

And I just need it to stop because it's all so loud.

Shoving the Grief Pangs is not working. YUSUF *grunts in frustration.*

Need something to drown it out. To feel solid.

YUSUF *notices the second cassette tape. He picks it up.*

Something's better than nothing.

YUSUF *puts the second tape in the player and presses play.*

Track Two

1996. 50 Wordsworth House, living room.

MUSTAFA. So they don't like it.

OMAR. I never said that /

MUSTAFA. / Basically what you're saying.

OMAR. Bro they said /

MUSTAFA. You weren't even there, how'd you know what they said?

OMAR. My cousin /

MUSTAFA. / Your cousin don't even work at Sony!

OMAR. Oi, rudeboy, relax yourself yeah. You know Mo?

MUSTAFA. Mo?

OMAR. Mo, bro, Mohammad.

MUSTAFA. I know what Mo stands for, yaar, *which* Mo? Lamba Mo?

OMAR *shakes his head.*

Chota Mo?

OMAR *shakes his head.*

OMAR. Mo who's flat got raided a couple months back. Mo from Stonebridge.

MUSTAFA. Say that then innit! What about him?

OMAR. I was at his mehndi on Sunday. So was my cousin and her Sony Records friend. They told me what the execs said.

MUSTAFA. How can they call that track 'risky'? What does that even mean?

OMAR. It means they don't understand that hip hop is resistance. You ain't even spitting about straps or brukking man up.

MUSTAFA. What else did they say?

OMAR. Leave it, Mus.

MUSTAFA. What did they say?

OMAR. Apparently, the execs don't think our music works in a club. Forget them, man, they're just budday goray who cares /

MUSTAFA. / We have to care, Omar. What they say goes innit? Do you see *any* apne in an exec position?

OMAR. That's why I'm studying business management, bro.

MUSTAFA. And I'm supposed to wait for you to finish uni, climb up the ranks? I'm not...

OMAR. Not what /

MUSTAFA. / I'm not smart like you. I can't do uni and them tings there. But I can do this.

OMAR. Mus, it ain't over. You think N.W.A stopped at the first no? We got a response. Which means they listened, which means we have their attention. So now, we hit 'em with the triple-touch method.

MUSTAFA. The what?

OMAR. It's a business ting. We reach out to a prospect, Sony Records, three times using different channels. Touch one – we sent them our first track. Touch two...

MUSTAFA. We send them another track! They think we can't do a club tune, let's make one.

OMAR. Wicked.

MUSTAFA. Touch three?

OMAR. Glad you asked, rudeboy. I went to the record shop today and saw this.

OMAR hands MUSTAFA a flyer.

MUSTAFA (*reading*). North West Sound Search?

OMAR. It's an open decks competition next week. Winner gets to record a track professionally at Abbey Road Studios!

MUSTAFA. Rah

OMAR. Bro, think about all the music managers that are gonna be there. Proper exposure! We invite Sony, that's touch three.

MUSTAFA. Rah

OMAR. You cool?

MUSTAFA. Bit nervous but fuck it yeah let's do it!

They do their handshake.

OMAR. It's a ten-minute set. You take care of the bars – I'll sort beats and logistics. Let's get cooking then!

MUSTAFA. Oi, about 'touch two'. I don't like this cousin shousin 'he said she said' shit.

MUSTAFA gets an envelope and pen, starts writing.

We're gonna put my address on this tape. 50 Wordsworth House. If those goray wanna chat about our music, they chat to us. (*Writing.*) 'Hip Hop is resistance. You ain't heard the last of us.' They think we can't make a club tune yeah? Ey, rudeboy, run that track.

The music kicks in. Rap mode activated. It should feel like a nightclub. Lights assist the storytelling of this track. The hook of this song should be sampled from a 90s Bollywood hit. There is room for choreography during the hook.

MUSTAFA.
>Bombay Jungle that is the scene
>Nightclub packed full of young desis
>Enter me Reeboks clean
>Scanning the room for a sweet lady
>
>Yo we come a long way from daytimer gigs
>Racists owners never used to let us in
>Now the brown pound pumping the brown sound
>Bombay Jungle Asian Underground
>
>Brown bodies bump to bhangra and Biggie
>Brown bodies bump in bombers and bindis
>Under lights I see her brown eyes
>Ruby-red dress with a slit for her thighs
>
>Under lights I'm hypnotised
>Walk in a trance to the middle of the dance
>In front of me this pyaari larki
>Takes my hand and with it, my heart
>
>*Hook.*
>
>Don't know her name but she sets the pace
>Drawn to her face we led by the bass
>Tumbis tumble with hi-hats as our
>Skin begins to make contact. Yo
>
>Our bodies fit like hands to a glove
>Word to Sade this no ordinary love
>Ruby-red dress has got me stressed like
>
>What can I say to make her impressed?
>Yo, my name is Double MC
>I'm tryna get in-between the seam of your jeans
>The way your body rolls is oh so wicked
>You stole my heart and my whole soul with it
>Number, name, time place
>And lemme know yo, can we kick it?
>She tuts, sighs, rolls her eyes
>'Chat better than that if you wanna get with it'
>
>*Hook.*

The girl of my dreams is making to leave
But like SRK in *DDLJ* I
Ain't gonna let this beauty get away so
I take a risk, take her wrist and say

Aap ki aankhon mein khwaabon pirthay hein
Aap ki saanson mein Shabnam aati hein
O soniye kabhi alvida na kehna
Agar aap nahein hai to mein marjaonga akela

Ruby-red dress looks impressed
I ask her to dinner the week after next
She takes my palm writes down an address
Leans in close says her name is Layla

Doctor-in-training eldest of five
In her eyes I see the rest of my life
Smile full of noor the brightest light
I lean in close and we kiss goodnight

Hook.

Scene Six

YUSUF *is at 50 Wordsworth House.* YUSUF *is centre-stage, stuck. He looks like he's just squashed another Grief Pang but hasn't been able to reset his body. He is completely tense – arms locked, legs straight, shoulders rounded – tense.*

YUSUF. Stuck.

Verb. One syllable. To be fixed in a particular position or unable to move or be moved.

I haven't moved. Supposed to call the council so the movers know when to take the boxes. Every time I think about Khalil it gets heavier and harder to move. My limbs are concrete pillars, can't shake it off.

Only thing that *was* taking my mind off Khalil was the tape. But now the stupid thing's not working and I don't know how to fix it! That tape, that track, is the story of how my parents met. Mustafa & Layla. But they weren't my parents then. They were just bodies shifting, shuffling, merging in the dark. That track brings more questions than answers. I want to call my mum, but time difference. Plus, she has a whole new life now, a family. [I don't want to bother her with this.]

I can't stop thinking about Mustafa, Layla, Omar – they all just knew how to be. Be themselves. How to dance like nobody's watching, sliding between English and Urdu, taking up space. I'm jealous.

Beat.

I don't know how to be – I'm stuck. Why did Khalil have to wear those badges and say the R-word in front of Paul?! Was he just trying to be vocal? Like Baba and Omar. How do I be that?

YUSUF *laughs to himself.*

'To be, or not to be, that is the question:
Whether 'tis nobler in the mind to suffer
The slings and arrows of outrageous fortune,
Or to take arms against a sea of troubles
And by opposing end them?'

I don't know the rest. It's not that simple. Coz unlike Hamlet, my sea of troubles doesn't start and end with me. And I can't even think about taking up arms without... I want to be able to say the R-word, wear the badges and ask Paul why there are only two authors of colour on our syllabus. But how? How do I say that without eyes burning into me. Without losing my job or being referred to Prevent? How do I be Muslim enough for my pupils, but not be too Muslim so my colleagues think I'm a threat? That is the question. Because working twice as hard, swallowing their little violences, letting them mispronounce my name isn't working. It doesn't feel noble. I'm stuck. And I'm pissed off because the one person who probably had the answers, who would know what to say, isn't here any more. Baba's not here any more, he's past-tense. And that makes me... sad.

Life and movement return to YUSUF*'s right arm. It surprises him.*

I'm sad.

YUSUF*'s left arm starts shaking, almost free.*

I'm upset.

YUSUF*'s left arm is free.*

I'm upset because I miss my baba, and I wish I knew him sooner.

YUSUF*'s torso and back is now free.*

That's it. Okay? I'm upset.

He tries to move but his legs are still stuck.

I'm upset.

He tries and fails again. Beat. He takes a big breath.

I'm upset and ashamed because I didn't attend my baba's funeral.

Yeah. But I tried, wallah I tried. I got to the mosque early like Dolly Aunty said. Just me, the man doing the Ghusl and Baba's body. And the man asked me to join in the Ghusl, to wash Baba's body before burial. And when I put my palm on Baba's forehead I jolted back because he was so cold. And I stared at him lying there. Silent. Still. A statue. All those other times he was sat right there I could've chatted, could've asked, could've bonded, but I didn't say anything. And the man from the mosque told me to carry on, that we had to wash him, but I couldn't. I couldn't. So I left and I walked and I didn't turn back. I came straight here and started packing.

YUSUF*'s limbs are free. His body is raw and wobbly.*

Now I'm meant to say goodbye when I'm just starting to know him.

The Grief Music returns but feels lighter.

YUSUF *moves and sorts the boxes. He does so with flow. The rigidity has left him. Time passes.*

Scene Seven

YUSUF *finishes moving and sorting boxes.*

DOLLY AUNTY. Oh, Yusuf, put the kettle on, beta!

YUSUF (*screams*). – "Salaam – how long have you been here?!"

DOLLY AUNTY. Long enough to see you fold clothes terribly.

YUSUF. "How did you get in?"

DOLLY AUNTY. I have key. Array, who do you think was checking in on your baba after you moved out?

YUSUF. "Right. Chai?"

DOLLY AUNTY (*nods*). Four sugars please.

YUSUF. I watch her, nestled on the sofa, and I clock how small she is. She's sat in Baba's spot running her hands over the worn leather. Baba was just sat on the sofa, until he wasn't. "Dolly Aunty, can I ask you something?"

She nods.

"Is your name actually Dolly?"

DOLLY AUNTY. Why you ask?

YUSUF. "I wanna know more about you, about Baba. I haven't been around much and –"

YUSUF*'s voice quivers.*

SCENE SEVEN 39

DOLLY AUNTY. Roh mat meri jaan. Okay, so even though I look like a doll... you're supposed to agree.

YUSUF. "Hahn yeah of course!"

DOLLY AUNTY. Even though I look like a doll, my name is actually Khadijah.

YUSUF. "Mashallah, beautiful name."

DOLLY AUNTY. Hahn, leyken when I first came here it was causing too many problems. My manager at sewing factory, she was gori. She would get so frustrated trying to pronounce my name. Her face would go red like a tamater! She would get so annoyed, she stopped speaking to me, just click and point. I thought maybe she will fire me. Back then I didn't wear hijab, my hair was big, bouncy and curly.

YUSUF. "Like Dolly Parton."

DOLLY AUNTY. Hahn! Pakistani Dolly Parton. To phir next day I march up to manager's office, show her picture of Dolly and say 'oi kutti ki bachi – call me Dolly' and it stuck.

YUSUF (*shakes his head*). "They can say Rebecca but not Khadijah. Both have three syllables."

DOLLY AUNTY. I know.

YUSUF. "And Khadijah is a strong name. Entrepreneur, first person to accept Islam, wife of the Prophet Muhammad (pbuh)."

DOLLY AUNTY. Array, we're not in school shool. I know this, beta. But Khadijah cause problem. Dolly is easy.

YUSUF. "I forgot to make chai."

DOLLY AUNTY. It's okay, not staying long. This is yours.

DOLLY AUNTY *pulls out a cassette tape from her pocket.*

Your baba wasn't always quiet.

YUSUF. "I know he used to rap."

DOLLY AUNTY. Hein? You know about the rapping shapping?

YUSUF. "Yeah, found the tapes in the suitcase."

DOLLY AUNTY. Ha! Saves me a lot of explaining.

YUSUF. "There are more tapes?"

DOLLY AUNTY (*shakes her head*). This is the last one. I took it when I came for Afsos. But then... you can't reach your baba's soul unless you know the truth. There's a reason he went quiet.

YUSUF *takes the cassette and puts it in the player. They listen together.*

Track Three

1996. Same living room. MUSTAFA *is sat with his notepad and pen.* OMAR *is prepping the decks.*

OMAR. Mus, I ain't tryna pressure you but /

MUSTAFA. / Then why you pressuring me?

OMAR. Competition's tomorrow, G, and we don't have a third track.

MUSTAFA. Don't you think I know that?

OMAR. I just need you to do your thing, man.

MUSTAFA (*mimicking*). That's not helping, man.

OMAR *approaches* MUSTAFA.

OMAR. Okay, chat to me. What's going on?

MUSTAFA. I don't know. I'm ready. But nothing's working! This has never happened before.

OMAR. It is weird.

MUSTAFA. I know!

OMAR. This condition usually happens to men over forty.

MUSTAFA. Ey what?

OMAR. Maybe you need some pills innit? Does Layla know?

MUSTAFA goes to hit OMAR.

Chill, man! So you've got writer's block, happens to every artist. Have sabr, bro.

MUSTAFA. Sabr? We ain't got time for sabr. Tomorrow's our chance. All the music execs. And if we don't. You're gonna go back to uni soon and then I'll just be stuck here.

Beat.

OMAR. Why do you rap?

MUSTAFA. What?

OMAR. Why d'you rap?

MUSTAFA. Coz it's sick, innit.

OMAR gestures/stays silent so MUSTAFA can be more honest.

Coz I love it

OMAR. Why?

MUSTAFA. Coz… I feel like a have a voice. Like we have a voice. Our culture, our struggle.

OMAR. Your bars start the conversation, G. That's what we're lacking.

MUSTAFA. What do you mean?

OMAR. We've just been surviving. Keeping our heads down when we walk past skinheads. Fighting National Front if they come near the blocks. That's just survival. Your words are our stories. They help us process what it means to be us. Muslim, Asian, British.

MUSTAFA. But that won't play on radio, they don't want that.

OMAR. Why does everything have to be for them? Your bars yeah... they make me feel good. About myself. Isn't that enough?

MUSTAFA. I want us to be more than good.

OMAR. Alright then, your bars make me feel invincible! Like I wanna quit my degree and do music full-time!

MUSTAFA turns to OMAR, smiling in surprise.

Obviously I ain't gonna do that, my mum would kill me. But the energy you have when you spit your truth? We need that.

OMAR gets out MUSTAFA's notepad, searches for a page.

MUSTAFA. What you doing?

OMAR. First thing you ever wrote. Let's record it.

Music kicks in. It's stripped back. Musical accompaniment to a spoken-word style piece.

MUSTAFA.
We are purposefully prideful perhaps to a fault
Power and positivity peruse our presence
Plenty permanently severed by partition
Still we persevere push purpose with our mission
Packaged within us, plethora of passions
Poets precariously pondering on politics
Passionate pehlwaans packing on pounds to smack man and spit paan
Punchy Punjabi to plush Pashdo
Our tongues contain more flavours than your
Problematic portrayals of our people
We are proof that persistence paves way for progress

We hear a medium-sized bang which momentarily distracts MUSTAFA and OMAR. The sound is not near them. They continue.

We are
An abomination on this 'great' nation
Archetypes of an archaic attitude

But actually we are actuaries accountants analysts academics actors and activists
Yet you assign us as the anarchist
Array yaar
Ain't you aware we have aspirational attributes in abundance?
And academically ain't anybody testing our ability
We are always aspiring for Azadi

We are kind we have never been far behind
Kohl kissed our skin before you lined your eyes
Kings and queens of keeping tradition alive
Coz our aunties are kebabs crackling with tenacity
Uncles, kulfi: cold yet comforting
The love for our khana is more united than this kingdom
Coz we are carrying knots you could never untie
Knots that can't be undone
We are carrying
Khubsoorat kahanis of our khandaan

Internationally known for a cricket team we hate to love and love to hate
Ignoring ignorance is daily but ignoring injustice
Is irrefutable incomprehensible
In our inner conscious
Identity is an interchangeable ideology
It inundates itself in our innermost thoughts
Irrespective of that we have to remember the fact that we are

Irre
Irre
Irreplaceable.

P-A-K-I
We are more than these four letters that you adore
There's a glossary attached to my ancestry
You choose to ignore each time –

We hear a loud bang and furious footfall. POLICE OFFICERS *have burst into the flat. Mic is dropped.* MUSTAFA *and* OMAR *react.*

OFFICER (*voice-over*). ON THE GROUND NOW! DON'T MOVE!

MUSTAFA *and* OMAR's *bodies reluctantly yet sharply submit to the brute force inflicted. Footfall continues, we hear objects being thrown as the flat gets raided.*

Anything? (*To* MUSTAFA *and* OMAR.) DON'T LOOK – (*To other officers.*) Alright. MOVE OUT!

The boys stay frozen and contorted as the footfall fades out. Until all we hear is their terrified breath.

Scene Eight

Back to the present. YUSUF *and* DOLLY AUNTY *have just finished listening to what we've seen.*

YUSUF. "But why?"

DOLLY AUNTY. I don't know. Maybe the police got hold of the tapes somehow and thought the music was suspicious? A lot of raids happened on this estate. I'm sorry, beta, but you deserve to know.

YUSUF. Suddenly everything makes sense but makes no sense. I feel sick. Dolly Aunty grips my hand. She tells me to hold on to the tapes, the jacket, the notepad, because that's who he was. At his core Baba was cheeky, badmaash, charming. In his soul. But they took away his voice. She says he didn't speak for a month, never returned Omar's calls and was paranoid every time a door slammed. Layla, my mum, thought he'd get over it because the man she met was strong. Thought maybe being a dad might bring him back. But his spirit was crushed. Mum couldn't stand to see him shrivel into silence, so she left. Dolly Aunty said he only grew colder and more distant. Impenetrable, like stone. And in the end, he felt most safe staring at the TV.

I look at Dolly Aunty, both our faces are wet. But I don't care. I'm spilling and that's okay. She tells me it's okay.

DOLLY AUNTY. I wish you saw him at the Janaza, beta. He looked so peaceful wrapped in white. For the first time in a long time, he wasn't carrying any of it.

YUSUF. We stay holding hands for I don't know how long. She holds my hand as I call the council and arrange a clearing date. Two weeks are almost up. She kisses my forehead and leaves.

Feel like I'm unravelling, but not in a bad way. The right way to be, it's been staring at me my whole life. In Dolly Aunty's cackle, Baba's bars. I've just been tuned in to the wrong frequencies. If you're always firm, you can never be fair.

YUSUF *walks over and picks up* MUSTAFA*'s notepad.*

They silenced Baba. They won't do the same to Khalil.

YUSUF *moves some boxes. Buttons up his shirt.*

Scene Nine

School. Internal exclusion room.

School bell rings.

YUSUF *sits opposite* KHALIL. KHALIL *is wearing a high-vis vest, fists and jaw clenched.*

YUSUF *holds* MUSTAFA*'s notepad.*

YUSUF. "Do you have to wear that the whole time?"

No response.

"You look like Bob the Builder"

KHALIL *shifts away.*

Probably not the right time to make jokes.

Too small to call this a classroom. Everything's grey. The table, chair, notebook and there's one window looking out to – you guessed it – a grey wall. Didn't even know school had a room like this.

"Khalil, I just wanna talk."

"I've been thinking a lot about what you said. And you were right, I was wrong."

KHALIL *shuffles, uninterested.*

"You were right about Hamlet. Hamlet is – extreme. And causes pain but nobody sticks that word on *him*, it's almost like it's reserved for – I'm getting off track. What I'm saying is… I'm sorry. I'm sorry for shutting you down when I should've heard you out. Truce?"

KHALIL *looks at* YUSUF, *whose hand is outstretched.*

KHALIL *shifts away.*

"I get it. I'm sorry you feel like you don't have permission. To speak. To have an opinion on Hamlet or any other character but that's the whole point you don't need permission you just need to know how to play the game. How *we* play the game" /

KHALIL. / We? Who's we?

YUSUF (*gestures*). "You and I, Musli– " /

KHALIL. / Did you get referred to Prevent?

YUSUF. "No."

KHALIL. Then *we* aren't in the same boat.

YUSUF. "Khalil, I want to help."

KHALIL. You've done enough.

YUSUF. "Please let me " /

KHALIL. / Let you what, trick me into getting expelled? They came to my house you know. These Prevent officers. Didn't look like Feds or teachers, something in-between. They didn't take their shoes off when they came in. And after they turned me and my brother's room upside down, they sat and told my parents that I was harbouring dangerous thoughts. That they were gonna monitor me. Make sure I don't become a threat.

YUSUF. "I had no idea."

KHALIL. Neither did my dad at first. See his English ain't that good. So I had to watch my ummi swallow all those things they said about me then spit it back out so Dad could understand. Ummi kept asking what crime I committed, and they couldn't give her a straight answer. Coz I haven't, have I? When they left and she asked me what crime I committed, I don't know. I felt so dirty on the inside. Couldn't speak. Didn't know if they could still hear me. I just wanted to be honest with Ummi. But I couldn't speak. And now I'm stuck here. Do you know why they make me wear this?

YUSUF. "Why?"

KHALIL. So it's easier for them to see if I attack you.

YUSUF. "Right."

KHALIL. I was meant to be the first one in the family to go uni. Can't be arsed to finish my personal statement now. First thing they'll see on my record is a Prevent referral, can't write myself out of that, can I? They probably won't even read it. All because you were too shook to call Hamlet what he is. I'm here because I said a word you didn't like.

YUSUF. "I – Your words are important, Khalil. You never know who they'll reach."

KHALIL. That's the point. If I speak, I'm scared of who it will reach.

YUSUF. His words just hang there. And as he stares, holding it all in, I see Baba. I see me. I see a young man on the verge of becoming a statue.

"When I was in Year 7, we were studying the crusades. And my teacher Miss Holt said Richard Lionheart, leader of the

English Christians, was 'brave' and Salahuddin, leader of the Muslims, was 'barbaric'. Brave. Barbaric. Both begin with B. Both mean different things. But both were fighting and killing. Both believed in defending something. But I was young, right. I remember walking home that day thinking 'brave' looks like Richard, fair skin blue eyes. Like Hamlet. 'Barbaric' looks like me. Like my dad. And that sticks. You become tangled up in it without realising. So it sticks with you at uni. And you start holding yourself to different standards, telling yourself to be a certain way just to prove you're not what the headlines say you are. You get so tangled up that years later you find yourself holding a remarkably intelligent seventeen-year-old boy to those impossible standards. All because he looks like you and prays like you. That's unfair. I'm sorry, Khalil. For being unfair to you, I should've known better. Should've known those standards are stickier than I thought. Even after reading Arundhati Roy and listening to Lowkey."

KHALIL. Lowkey's cold.

YUSUF. "Yeah, he is! All I've wanted to do is collect and dissect words so gifted young people like you can free yourselves. So ten years from now your bars are the ones freeing others. But maybe I lost sight of that. You've taught me something, you know."

KHALIL. Swear?

YUSUF (*nods*)."That *we* must actively untangle ourselves from the language this dunya sticks on us."

Beat. KHALIL *agrees.*

"I thought we'd forget Hamlet for a bit and look at some contemporary work. I think you'll resonate with this, especially since you're a poet."

KHALIL. Spoken-word artist.

YUSUF *smiles, acknowledging the correction as he passes Mustafa's notepad to* KHALIL. KHALIL *reads.*

Ey these are cold! Double MC, is he on TikTok?

YUSUF. "Nah, he's old-school."

KHALIL. Did you know him then?

YUSUF. "I wish I did. (*About the notepad.*) How does it make you feel?"

KHALIL. Impressed. This one about the P-word, all that imagery from dissecting one word.

YUSUF. "Makes you realise how loaded words can be."

KHALIL. But reading it kinda changes how the word lands.

YUSUF. "How?"

KHALIL. It ain't as heavy. Coz this guy, Double MC, he's scooped up – he's *untangled* all the thoughts I have about that word and laid it out. Makes me feel seen.

YUSUF. "How?"

KHALIL. Are you just gonna keep saying 'how'?

YUSUF *smiles and shrugs, waiting for* KHALIL *to expand.*

Double MC uses assonance and alliteration to pick apart the P-word. Kinda like disassembling a gun. Instead, he fills each stanza with joyful, culturally rich imagery. Expanding what it means to be Pakistani. So you read it and you feel bigger. Bigger than the P-word.

YUSUF *opens* KHALIL*'s notepad to a blank page.*

YUSUF. "Tell you what, creative writing is on your exam so let's practice. Write me something similar."

KHALIL. What?

YUSUF. "Pick a word you want to untangle yourself from. Disassemble it. See what happens, I'll set the timer."

KHALIL *starts to write.*

I watch him write. His eyes focused only on the space between the lines. Ears shut off from all the noise and I think 'is this enough?' These ten minutes to express, where he feels unbound. Is it okay if that's enough? Because how can I actually create change while we're trapped in a cage of oppression? When I don't have enough change to afford change? Is this small win enough? I watch him right, and he's smiling like there's nobody watching. Wrist flicking ink. Now I'm smiling. And I realise you can't contain joy. It's contagious, it must be shared.

"Okay time's up, finish the sentence you're on."

KHALIL. Sir, just one more minute!

YUSUF. "Can't ask the invigilator for one more minute. Bas, let me see."

YUSUF *reads, he's moved.*

KHALIL. It's rubbish innit, just say it.

YUSUF. "Khalil this is… it's… radical."

They share a smile. KHALIL's *face changes. He tears the page off the notepad and offers it to* YUSUF.

KHALIL. Sir, can you take it for now.

YUSUF. "If I take that, I'd be telling you to stay quiet."

KHALIL. In case they check it.

YUSUF. "I'll take it. But something as brilliant as this doesn't deserve to be kept quiet. Come see me at the end of the day, I'll give it back to you. The louder we are, Khalil, the harder it is to be silenced."

School bell rings.

"I better get going. Really great work today."

YUSUF *packs* MUSTAFA's *notepad and makes to leave.*

KHALIL. Ey, sir… you're a good teacher, you know.

YUSUF. "Say mashallah innit."

Scene Ten

KHALIL*'s bedroom.* KHALIL *has set up his phone to record a video. He is holding the piece of paper containing his freewrite from the previous scene.*

KHALIL. Got a new piece for you lot, fresh off the dome.
Shout-out Mr Malik, shout-out Double MC. The louder we are the harder it is to silence us! Aight boom:

Clears his throat.

How to pronounce: Radical
Curve the tip of your tongue upwards
Revving your vocal engine
Push the edges of your lips away
Opening wide to consume headlines
A satisfying shred of a skateboard/surfboard/snowboard/
Object which mostly white men stand on top of
Forget whiteboards were meant to be written on
Bill and Ted's catchphrase:
Rad

Nickname for Richard
Because that makes more sense
Than stretching your jaw
To house the second vowel
Already written in my name
Border Force officer
Hands firmly clasped on vest
Knuckles saying something with their chest
Male phallus:
Dic

Pretense in Arabic language
Knighting adjective into noun
Short for Alistair
Coz all they do is stare
Once they clock skin tone, backpack and facial hair
Remove a crown of your own jewels

Replace it with knuckles
That dig into your temple:
Al

Radical
Three syllables that make
Bruddas shudder
Under sunlight
Radical

KHALIL *stops filming and we leave his bedroom.* YUSUF *repositions boxes until they are evenly spaced out in a straight line. From one of the boxes he takes out a backpack and puts it on.*

Scene Eleven

YUSUF*'s phone is buzzing from messages and notifications. He doesn't answer. Buzzes stop. We don't know it yet, but* YUSUF *is at Carpenders Park Lawn Cemetery.*

YUSUF. Dolly Aunty said it was the one next to the one with flowers… they all have flowers!

YUSUF *gets out his phone.*

Ah, she said pink flowers. Oh. Three missed calls from Paul.

Later.

I didn't have signal the whole time I was on the Overground. What's the point of having the Overground if you get no signal?

He takes in his surroundings, trying not to spiral into avoidance.

Carpenders Park.

YUSUF *walks carefully. He does not walk directly past a box, instead walking a rectangular path around each one.*

Still searching.

It is nice, mashallah. Green. Quiet. Graveyards always are, though, aren't they? Even the wind stands still in respect.

YUSUF's *phone buzzes again.*

My phone is – I was gonna say 'blowing up' but I'm [cautious] – nah bun it. My phone is blowing up!

YUSUF *gets out his phone and reads his notifications.*

Five emails from Paul all with the red exclamation mark. He's copied in HR. Oh. Khalil posted his poem on TikTok, ten thousand views since last night. Work wants to know why Khalil gave me a shout-out.

YUSUF *gulps.*

Beat. Conflicted. Tempted. Nervous.

Later.

Ah! Pink flowers.

Beat. YUSUF *is standing in front of his baba's grave for the very first time.*

Part of me wants to dive in and hope the soil isn't real.

So I can see you.

You know, if I'd have known you rapped, I would've told them to put Double MC on the headstone.

YUSUF *takes a deep breath. An honest one.*

Baba, I –

Phone buzzes again. YUSUF *takes it out and –*

Flight mode.

It's chilly.

YUSUF *unzips his bag, taking out Mustafa's jacket and putting it on.*

Hope you don't mind, Ba.

The movers are coming tomorrow. Dolly Aunty will be there. We both will. It'll be nice, to say goodbye together.

I'm sorry I –

YUSUF *notices a strange sensation from within, he half-raises his arms in half-surprise.*

I feel fuzzy and floaty. And a little nauseous.

YUSUF *breathes, settles into this sensation.*

Nah this feels nice. Feels like someone is hugging my heart from the inside.

YUSUF *notices his arm position. He brings his hands close, cupping them for Dua. He recites the following.*

Bismillah irrahman nirrahim
Rabbir hamhuma kama Rabbayani Sagheera
Rabbir hamhuma kama Rabbayani Sagheera
Rabbir hamhuma kama Rabbayani Sagheera

Ameen.

Hope you don't mind if I stay for a while, Baba, there's a lot we need to unpack.

The new Grief Music breezes in. Traces of the old music are there, but this one feels more manageable. This one has more love in it.

End.

Urdu Glossary

Baba	Dad
Daadi	Grandmother
Astaghfirullah	May Allah forgive me
Gora/Gori	White man/White woman
Surah	Chapter in the Quran
Array	Oi
Badmaash	Naughty/Hooligan
Bakwaas	Rubbish
Baat khattam	End of discussion
Beta	Son
Meri Jaan	My life (a term of affection and endearment. Equivalent to 'my dear')
Dunya	World
Mazak	Jokes
Dua	Prayer
Yaar	Mate
Lamba	Tall
Chota	Small
Wallah	Swear to God
Ghusl	Islamic ritual of prepping a corpse for funeral. Ablution of the corpse performed by immediate relation of same gender
Roh mat	Don't cry
Hahn	Yes!
Kutti ki bachi	Daughter of a bitch
Janaza	Funeral
Mashallah	'What Allah has willed'. A praise of respect. To denote something great has happened.
Leyken	But
To phir	So then

Bismillah irrahman nirrahim
With the name of Allah, the most gracious the most merciful
Rabbir hamhuma kama Rabbayani Sagheera
'My Lord, have mercy upon them as they brought me up (when I was) small.' (Quran 17:24)

A Nick Hern Book

Statues first published in Great Britain as a paperback original in 2024 by Nick Hern Books Limited, The Glasshouse, 49a Goldhawk Road, London W12 8QP in association with Two Magpies Productions and the Bush Theatre, London

Statues copyright © 2024 Azan Ahmed

Azan Ahmed has asserted his right to be identified as the author of this work

Cover photography by Harry Elletson

Designed and typeset by Nick Hern Books, London
Printed in Great Britain by Mimeo Ltd, Huntingdon, Cambridgeshire PE29 6XX

A CIP catalogue record for this book is available from the British Library

ISBN 978-1-83904-403-8

CAUTION All rights whatsoever in this play are strictly reserved. Requests to reproduce the text in whole or in part should be addressed to the publisher.

Amateur Performing Rights Applications for performance, including readings and excerpts, by amateurs in the English language should be addressed to the Performing Rights Manager, Nick Hern Books, The Glasshouse, 49a Goldhawk Road, London W12 8QP, *tel* +44 (0.)20 8749 4953, *email* rights@nickhernbooks.co.uk, except as follows.

Australia: ORiGiN Theatrical, *tel* +61 (2.) 8514 5201, *email* enquiries@originmusic.com.au, *web* www.origintheatrical.com.au

New Zealand: Play Bureau, 20 Rua Street, Mangapapa, Gisborne 4010, *tel* +64 21 258 3998, *email* info@playbureau.com

USA and Canada: The Artists Partnership, see details below.

Professional Performing Rights Applications for performance by professionals in any medium and in any language throughout the world should be addressed to The Artists Partnership, 21–22 Warwick Street, London W1B 5NE, *tel* +44 (0)20 7439 1456, *email* email@theartistspartnership.co.uk

No performance of any kind may be given unless a licence has been obtained. Applications should be made before rehearsals begin. Publication of this play does not necessarily indicate its availability for amateur performance.

www.nickhernbooks.co.uk/environmental-policy

www.nickhernbooks.co.uk

facebook.com/nickhernbooks

twitter.com/nickhernbooks